Time 2 MANning Up

Jasper "Mr. HORSE" Manning

WESTBOW
PRESS®
A DIVISION OF THOMAS NELSON
& ZONDERVAN

WestBow Press books may be ordered through booksellers or by contacting:

WestBow Press
A Division of Thomas Nelson & Zondervan
1663 Liberty Drive
Bloomington, IN 47403
www.westbowpress.com
1 (866) 928-1240

ISBN: 978-1-9736-7825-0 (sc)
ISBN: 978-1-9736-7826-7 (hc)
ISBN: 978-1-9736-7824-3 (e)

Library of Congress Control Number: 2019916867

Print information available on the last page.

WestBow Press rev. date: 11/15/2019

Contents

Dedication

This book is dedicated to those who have passed before me, and
Because of their love and sacrifice I am the man I am today.

Acknowledgement

1st, give praise and all honor to God, who I came to know at an early age. He was introduced to me by my mom Alice Faye Carter-Manning-Raye. My inspiration for this book comes from her as well as my son's Jasper E. Manning II, Jaelen Earl Manning and wife Sophia Londe Manning. I'm also inspired by a host of other relatives for their love and the way in which they lived their lives. Sharing and demonstrating their wisdom, disciplines, traditions, loyalty and commitment to family that I've recalled or referenced at some point or another in the writings of this book.

Inspiration:
Edwina Carter, Nathaniel Carter, Melvin Carter, Alice Fay Carter, Olin Ray Carter, Nathaniel Carter, Marie Carter, Phillip Earl Carter, Wank Tippens, Ruth Ann Tippens, Mariah Yarber, Anne Pearl Yarber, Socrates Yarber, Lovie Yarber, Johnnie Yarber, Maggie Mae Manning, Yuteen Manning, Woodrow Manning, Earnestine Manning, Neil Manning, Ora Mae Carter, Bessie Mae Carter, Juanita Carter, Bessie Mae Carter, Juanita Carter, Mack Earl Tippens, Anne Pearl Carter, Judy Tippens.

I hope that you're blessed as much as I have been in your lives and your walk with GOD when reading some of the poems and the meanings behind them.

Enjoy and thanks for your support in trying to help me leave things better than I found them. Embrace the world and all that God has meant for it to be.

Introduction

Our society has come to disregard the principals of civility over the course of my adult life which hasn't been that long. Some of us have even forgotten the sacrifices needed to instill values in our children so that they may grow to be productive young adults and continue to nurture the seeds of life. I don't have it all figured out, but I think that I'm on the right track. If I offend you then you're the one this book was written for because you are part of the problem. If it doesn't offend you then help me leave things better than we found them.

GOD's grace may not be touching the lives of everyone yet, but he is still out present and available for all to embrace. It is hard to recognize and embrace GOD because of so many false prophets that choose to disrupt rather than deliver. I'm not prophet but God has been good to my wife and I, and we would like to share those blessings when anyone who needs a blessing.

CHAPTER I

What Man

Earlism:

1.

LIVE LIFE TODAY
SO THAT TOMORROW
YOU'RE NOT ASHAMED
OF WHAT YOU DID YESTERDAY

Daddy-Less-Ness

I saw a little boy in school one day
He seemed troubled and distraught
I asked if he had a dad at home
He's in jail because, he got caught

He had a look that possessed his face
With an explanation he hated to give.
How's a kid to be successful in life?
When he feels he has no reason to live?

He's always into something
And I must speak to him everyday
His mom is doing the best she can
I hate bothering her every single day

So, while at school I would check on him
To see how things are that day
Now he seems to smile a little more
And his teachers have good things to say

Now when I see him in the hall
He seems to smile a little bit more
With a special hand shake this kid and I
One he's never shared before

It's been a while since his smile
I hope he is graduation bound
Trusting the lasting relationships
Would leave things better than found

At the end of the Day

At the end of the day
All you have is your word
Whether you lie, cheat or steal
What you do is all they heard

They say the essence of a man's thoughts
Are a man's actions
There should be full accountability
Of a man's integrity not a fraction

Do what you say
And say what you mean
In today's time we must strive
For excellence, started from a dream

So, at the end of the day
Challenge if you may
The thoughts of sacrifice and perception

We're past the skin
That comes up now and thin
Still you must be the exception

So, at the end of the day
All you have is what you say
So, when people stop listening to you
They should see what you're trying to say

A Valuable Life

Giving you what you want
Is not giving you what you need
This type of family support
Can only lead to envy and greed

A hard day's work
A value that has become lost
At the end of a lifetime
What can truly be the cost?

Where will that leave you?
When support is dead and gone
It's hard to live a life in love
When you're raised to be alone

When you save for what you want
And work for what you need
It will be easy to live your life
When taught how to succeed

Everyone has a choice in life
Of the way it's going to end
Work hard and save your money
Or its integrity you'll one day spend

Angry Young Man

Poor little angry child
Caught up in a lie
He's so busy living the past
That life will pass him by

Go to bed to wake up later
The last 10 years were fake
Don't know whether to laugh or cry
So, its havoc that he creates

His mom won't take the time
To watch him grow as a child
An anger hidden deep within
Sometimes it's hard to smile

Someone will need teach him
And take him by the hand
An angry child with a closed mind
Will never grow to understand

Not knowing about love
So, he's quick to fight.
No one to tell him it's okay
And that things will be alright

He wears his small clothes baggy
Just to try and fit in
Not knowing that a real leader
Set their own trend

I pray someone takes his hand
And shows this young man the way
If he continues this angry path
He won't live to see another day

Bigger, Better You

Everyone has a dream
To be bigger than they are
But if you really think about it
You're fine being you thus far

Don't take the act
Don't take the pretend
Don't take the lie
You know where you've been

It really doesn't matter
What other people may think
Because you can choose to float
Or you may choose to sink

So just be your self
You can't tell God what to choose
Do what's right day or night
And in life you'll never loose

If for some reason you think
That being you is tough
If you're not enough with you
Without; you will never be enough

Because when you really look at
You're already bigger than you were
Because this poem made you think
The real you, is what you'd prefer

Broken Pieces

People may find a broken piece
And tend to throw them away
They can't see beyond their eyesight
So, they dispose of it that day

Never taking the time to realize
Any broken piece can be fixed
Some of the things you used today
Repairable items still do the trick

What do we do with people?
Whom we feel are already broke?
Do we simply through them away?
Thinking that this must be a joke

What about their value
The whole vessel can't be condemned
Why is it even hard for Christians?
To see there's still good in them

Everyone in this world is broke
With one crack larger than the other
This world would be a place of misfits
If no one cared or bothered

God didn't give up on us
When his son died on the cross
So, if God cared enough to save us
Why do you count us out as a loss?

If you and I are broken pieces
Why can't we mend our ways?
Fixing things that we find wrong
Will lead to more mended days

In my America

In my America
Slavery did exist
I thought we moved on
A time no one will miss

Humanity has a place
Where decency survives
I want what others want
To live and be alive

Wake up in the morning
To love what God's done
Creating souls young and old
Guess what, I was one

Sharing dreams of a King
In a nation, still asleep
Every day that I awake
Hearts alive still weep

Justice cries, opened eyes
So, blind she'll no longer be
Fathom crime is equitable
It's not just people like me

I don't see the hate
When hate is what they seek
People won't speak to you
So, to them I will speak

I pray in time we will find
A way to co-racially exist
Lincoln said before died
There'll be no co-racial bliss

Buoyantly in my America
One day I will rise
To see a day, I can say
America finally opened its eyes

The Needy

I want her in my life
Because I need her from time to time
I need her to calm my thoughts
And sooth my peace of mind

I need her to walk with me
When my mind needs fresh air
I need her to hold her hand
When she thinks that no one cares

I need her when the sun comes up
And when it begins to descend
I need her to tell this story
From the beginning to our end

I need her to trust me
So that together we can over come
Whatever the world throws at us
We can handle all of that and then some

I need her to love me
The way that I will love her back
I want her to have the world
Move forward and never look back

I need her to pray with me
Morning noon and night
So that our kids embrace life
And symbolize what's wrong and right

I need her to need me
To touch the pain inside
Put there by someone else
Who will no longer make her cry?

Most of all I need her patience
Because I won't always get it right
I'll do my best to help her rest
As she lays down to sleep at night?

To Tell the Truth

The truth is often told
From the perspective of the winner
Somewhere between the lines
The truth at times get thinner

What really happened who was there
No one will truly know.
All we have is that one perspective
With little evidence to show.

Some will hide the truth forever
Until their dying day
Then come out 50 years later
Now with something to say.

Dr. Martin Luther King Jr
Didn't die from a gunshot womb
He died from the smother of a pillow
A doctor sealed his doom

They let our America think
Dr. King died on that ledge
They knew what the truth would do
Divide a country with a racial wedge

It hurt the country to the core
To find out how Dr. KING died.
Who knows what history to believe
When parts of the country lied.

We're force to learn a history
That deep down doesn't sound right.
So they get a chance to tell their truth
When lies are right in our sight.

That Winning Hand

Some kids are dealt a hand
That life won't let them win
Surrounded by the trouble of the world
Failing over, and over again

Every day seems the same
Wake up; misery; go to bed
Not knowing how to appreciate life
Without dreams their already dead

They find it easier to just not try
Disguised by laughter and wit
It is what it is, is what they say
When all along they're ready to quit

Talking back with disrespect
Thinking it makes them grown
After a while, there is no child
Because now they're on their own

They run, they jump, and laugh
When they play
School is their only way out
For some the best part of their day?

There's no sign of support at home
Its grandma, drugs, or jail
Alternative school begins to rule
Failure comes without fail

When their lights go out at night
These are their hopes and dreams?
This is not the way life is
But to them it's the way life seems

To look in their eyes and see no hope
Can really melt the heart
Playing life with a losing hand
A hand dealt from the start

This Man

Earlism:

2.

If you're not leading the way
Then you're in the way.

When She Leaves

When she leaves in the morning
I know she's coming back
Sometimes I hate to see her go
Later I won't know how to act

We laugh joke poke fun at each other
as soon as she walks through the door
We ask each other about our day
Then cut up with each other some more

She seems to know what I'm thinking
Before the words ever come out
And just by the look on her face
She's upset sharing what it's about.

Then we have our times to chill
Just glad to be at home
We enjoy the company of others
But there's nothing like being alone

Then when we lay it down at night
We don't just go right to sleep
Not unless we're both dead tired
So quiet, not a word, not a peep

Don't wake her up if she's tire
Because now you've poked the bear
She says that sleep is the new sex
But I'm not trying to hear that there

Ending a sentence with a preposition
Isn't something I'd normally do?
But if you were married to my wife
Then you'd be crazy happy too.

The Beauty of a Woman

The beauty of a woman
Is evident when she walks
With every fiber of her being
It comes out when she talks

You can tell by the way she looks
Confidence is in the room
Then her smile carries for miles
Disparaging any form of gloom

The way she holds her head
When swinging it all around
Then the look that follows the turn
Shackling emotions to calm down

Whenever she begins to speak
You hang on to every word
Even when it brings familiarity
It's like nothing you've ever heard

With every woman there's a scent
Hormones that harm the senses
In those moments of intimacy
The passion becomes relentless

When passion ends emotions begin
It's when that moment comes to rest
Then in the mind that moment in time
You didn't expect anything less

Now the beauty of this woman
Will carry forward in time
With every chance, close your eyes
The beauty of this woman is mine

A Toast to You

What does happy feel like?
Let me share the way I feel
I met my wife on Zoosk.com
And I thought to myself what a steal

None were able to step it up
So, it was she who passed over them
Then when she got to my profile'
She looked and said "This is Him"

So, at night before we lay it down
Our issues are put to rest
Not because we entertain issues
But when in love you give it your best

We pray before each meal
And in this life, it is a must
God answered our prayers with a yes
And in him we trust

She makes me smile when she smiles
When I don't feel like smiling
Her concerns are my concerns
Even when she thinks I'm denying

I can't wait to touch her
Even if it's just to touch her hand
I touch her laughter with my eyes
For a committed heart understands

I can't wait for what comes next
Because alike are the greatest of minds
In our hands we choose where to stand
Because God made this time our time.

Dedicated to
My Friend, My Wife, My Love, My Life

You remind me of Love

Out goes the old
And in comes the grew
Skies once grey
Are now sky blue?

Whenever I take a drink
I can taste your lips
So, to embrace your breath
I drink in little sips

Every song I hear
Reminds me of things we did
Warmth and love in a candy store
Can you believe it, I'm the kid?

The scent of your excitement
Comes along with every breeze
When I'm with you all I want
Is the wish to please?

When leaves blow along the ground
I'm reminded of your hair
Then I just close my eyes
And in that breeze, I'm right there

Sometimes I can hear you call
When walking all alone
Before I can turn to answer
The sound of your voice is gone

I can feel a sense of love
I'm reminded of every day.
Sense I love her so much
My sense of love will stay

A Smile that'll melt the World

I married to a beautiful lady
With a smile that'll melt the world
A smile that's produced magic
Since she was a little girl

Whenever she'd smile
Her dad found ways to spoil her
So, who am I to tell her no?
When she smiles, I just deliver

Whenever she smiles
People just seem to smile back
A smile that comes from the heart
You can tell it's not an act

Whenever it's hard for her to smile
Everybody seems to know
She doesn't feel well at all
Still she smiles to say hello

The way she holds her head
Emphasizes what she feels
If she holds her head to the side
Her happiness is for real

If she holds her head up high
Her smile is to meet and greet
If her head is held down low
She's not just looking at your feet

She has a smile to melt the world
But that's not her better half
If you want to see a change in the world
Then you should hear her laugh

Alice Fay Carter Manning

It's been more than 20 years
Since my mom passed away
There's not a moment that goes by
She doesn't cross my mine in some way

Her love, leadership, and guidance
And the way she did certain things
Cook, clean, and worshipped God
Then on Sunday's in church she'd sing

She loved us all very much
But each love came with underwritten terms
All of us required a different hand
Served with pride as she was firm

My brother needed a firm hand
And we all needed her prayer
My sister needed I don't know
Whatever mom's and daughter's share

I think I needed
A firm hand too
I got so many whippings
For the things I was going to do

But at the end of the night
We knew where love was laid
Making sure we got what was needed
No matter how often mom got paid

So, God rest her soul
For its peace she finally found
I pray I serve her memory correct
Because I never want to let her down

Before we met

Before we had a chance to meet
This poem was written for you
About how amazing you'd be
And the magical things you'd do

You'd brighten up an entire room
Just by the way you laugh
Hearty and healthy full of joy
You'd be anyone's amazing half

Style, grace the way you'd walk
Would have a presence any place
Your emotions are your wardrobe
Worn by the accessories, on your face

There can never be an excuse
About the person you've become
People can tell just by your character
The type of place you came from

God took the good things in life
And placed them in your heart
Love compassion and gentleness
Those are just the standard parts

He took these special emotional traits
That only a God can do
Placed them in someone for the reason
I knew you before I ever met you

Blissful Relationship

One of the perks of a relationship
Is to build dreams and memories
The best way to get started is to
Do things together that please

Cooking dinner by candlelight
Send her flowers at work
Sitting outside on the porch at night
When the birds singing in chirps

Holding hands at the movies
Popcorn and a drink
Lay her head on your shoulder
Not worried what people think

Riding downtown with the top down
Moon beaming in her eyes
She wakes up in the middle of the night
So happy she smiles and sighs

You find yourself pushing a cart
At a store as she shops
A love that seems so unreal
You never want it to stop

You finish sentences as you speak
Catch her eye across a room
You picture her in a long white dress
Her the bride and you the groom

Now comes time to pop the question
Kneeling to one knee
Look in her eyes before she cries
Will you please marry me?

Flowers, rice and long white veil
With items all over her head
Look back at life and the other wife
It should have been her instead

But that's not how God planned it
Now your time has come to pass
To live laugh and love each other
Like it's never going to last

To sum it all up in this relationship
You get to do it everyday
Lifelong friends until the end
It started from the very first day

Female Kryptonite

My woman is my weakness
When it comes down to it
I'll do everything to protect her
I don't have a problem proving it

If there's top secret information
Please don't tell my wife
Because if something happens to her
I would gladly risk my life

If a car in coming out of control
I would push her out of the way
Then I'd try to save myself
To live to love another day

Our family is our reason to live
And the reason we survive
There's nothing is this world like love
To make you feel alive

Don't ask me anything about her
You don't need to know
Because if you can't get with this
Then you will have to go.

So, if you don't want to see the EARL
Then please don't mess with her
Cause I'll do whatever it takes
To protect and defend her

Grass Land

What do you see when you look at grass?
Is it the lawn of a lifetime?
It may not be the people's choice lawn
But this lawn is all mine.

All you do is water it daily
Make sure the grass never thirsts
Cut it, trim it, and keep it well groomed
That's because your yard comes first

I've seen people neglect their yards
Grass sprouting up weeds
Watering their grass once a week
When their yard had a greater need

The lack of water can make a yard dry
Where the ground will eventually crack
Too much heat, too much pressure
Too far gone, to never come back

Even if it decides to grow
The grass will never be the same
If your yard refuses to blossoms
You're the one to blame

So, you try to get another yard
But the same thing happens again
Why get a new yard if you don't work hard
To keep it from happening again

In order to keep grass beneath your feet
Don't walk on it any kind of way
With love, water and proper care
That grass will be green everyday

Miles of Heart

My dear sweet Aunt Hattie
She was one of God's seed
She was here for a reason
To ensure we'd all succeed

All my Aunts stayed with her
At one point or another
Their families made it through
She taught them how to be mothers

Now she's getting up in age
As women God sent usually do
If you ever came across her
I'm sure she touched your life too

I saw her just the other day
On her 92nd birthday
She still knew how to laugh
Which she did a lot that day?

I just can't help to think
Where would I be without Aunt Hattie?
She's a big part of the reason
Of the man I've grown to be

I have some stories
That I could really tell you
About whippings and how I grew up
It's amazing I made it through

When I look into her eyes
I get a reality check
A woman whose life was meaningful
Hattie Miles earned my respect

A lifetime filled with love
A kindness we should've learned
To love and take care of each other
As she did, now it's our turn

Mom Memories

I was at a laundry mat
And it brought back a memory
Of a child helping his mother fold clothes
That's what my mom meant to me
The child was very manner able
Clean cut and dressed nice
His pants were pulled up
No slang I had to look twice

He was twelve years old
Just him and his mom
Mine did the same for me
So, I knew where he was coming from

She taught me how
To wash earn and fold
And to this day
Cooking for me never gets old

I've done the same for my son's
Self-sufficiency is a must
I won't always be around
Rearing is what they will trust

It was good to see this young man
Help his mom instead of in the streets
This may have been Friday the 13th
But today my spirit received a treat

My Best Friend

I've waited all my life
To find my best friend
Someone to share everything
Especially until the very end

Someone who gets me
And me them too
She'd know my weaknesses
Because that's what friends do

They amplify your strengths
So, we can be successful
They love you anyway
And never appear resentful

Whenever you need it to be
Everything seems just right
It never matters when you need them
It can be either day or night

They love you at your worst
And appreciate you at your best
Friends are friends forever
Because you both deserve the best

Then when all is said and done
Done is what we'll be
I want to marry my best friend
A friend who knows how to love me

My Warrior Princess

My baby rode a bicycle
Just to make ends meet
When she didn't have a car
She used her head and feet

You don't find women like that
A warrior just for the cause
Not expecting anything in return
No pat on the back and no applause

She does what has to be done
Because it must be done
This Princess a pillar of strength
Just this woman and her son

He knows who God is
Because she showed him the way
By the way she lives her life
Every single day

Her knowledge in beyond the classroom
I love and admire her mind
She has learned so much in life
In such a short amount of time

This is the kind of woman
I want by my side
For if she decides to take this trip
We will all enjoy the ride

One Special Night

She stood up and stood out
Online and in a crowd
After talking to her on the phone
I know that mom would be proud

I was afraid to come here tonight
After talking to her on the phone
I've never been in love at first sight
But I felt I won't have to live life alone

There was something in her voice
That kept my attention engaged
It was just her and I; talking
No lights, no camera, no stage

We have so much in common
And just to name a few
We're both Libra's
And I'm 4 days older than you

I've always heard of love at first sight
But never believed it to be true
That has suddenly all changed
Because tonight I met you

Of all the places in the world
I would have never thought to look
She graduated from Dunbar high school
You can no longer hide in that book

You'll never have to worry
About where you stand with me
Because by your side always
Is where I will want to be?

I could tell from her tone
Her demeanor wasn't an act
So, tonight I'll make this promise to you
If you love me, I'll love you back

In My Shoes

I've worn many pairs of shoes
Over the years and time
I'll bet none of your shoes
Fit you like mines fit mine

I've worn the shoes of happiness
That fit oh so well
Then I had the kind of shoes
So broke you couldn't tell

Let me start with happiness
Where everything fell into place
There wasn't anywhere I couldn't go
My feet would move with grace

God woke me up in the morning
And shadowed me during the day
No matter where I seem to walk
God has always provided a way

Even when the days were dark
Walking along that path
My steps just seem to line up
I don't know you do the math

Then there were the days
When racism covered my shoe
A stranger to my siblings and I
Growing up we didn't have a clue

South Oak Cliff, my high school
Black students from door to door
If we were called the N' word
It never registered to us before

I was in our nation's Air Force
When I was called this 'N' word
It took a white guy to call out
For this word to be finally heard

Now this word had a new meaning
I vowed to never use the N word again
For the very 1st time I saw the world
Through the eyes of a black man

That Question

I had a student in the 6th grade
She touched my heart one day.
She asked me a powerful question
I struggled to find words to say.

To protect the student's identity
I cannot call her name
She almost brought my eyes to tears
But that day it didn't rain

She asked me a question
I wasn't ready to answer but did
Why doesn't God like me?
As she dazed upon the other kids

It took me a moment to answer
But the words finally came
God is wanting to make you stronger
His glory will be proclaimed

He won't take us through things
Without having a plan in place
He likely used you to remove them
From another time and place

She appeared to be a happy child
But she did have her days
Family members took her innocence
She found reasons to smile anyway

That question caught me by surprise
Provoking grateful thoughts
Our mom protected us from the world
A price not easily bought

I think about this student
I wonder about her from time to time
I often pray that everyday
My answer brought peace of mind

That Man

Earlism:

3.
Sometimes
Being good enough
Isn't good enough.
You've got to be BETTER.

A Better You
A Better Me

Have you ever met someone?
Who made you want to be a better you?
Things seem to be a little different
Things you didn't think you'd do

The sky seems a little bluer
And the air seems extra clean
The water seems purer on the lake
Car rides are longer than seemed

A whole new world
Begins to pour from her eyes
Suddenly everything has an answer
Questions are no longer whys

When you close your eyes at night
Dreams start and they end
Fantasies are now closer to touch
Where hearts can now transcend

You're nervous when around her
And your hands begin to sweat
Careful with the words you chose
Like no one else you've ever met

This is the type of person
That for years men overlook
They fail to see her true value
These pages, in this brand-new book

Thumbing back through the book of life
At the things you used to do
You find a way to commonly say
At times she felt just like you.

A Man Who Will Love You

Don't be afraid of love
A man that will love you
A man that will hold you
But won't try to control you

A man who will see
The things that you don't see
A man to be who you need him to be
Without being told what to be

A man who will listen
To whatever you have to say
Even if it comes out wrong
He'll listen to you anyway

A man who will take the lead
And walk with you side by side
He's not afraid to share his dreams
That you both deserve inside

Then when it's all over
And the day comes to an end
Know that he'll be there with you
To keep and protect you again

A man that will love you
Will feel your pain before you do
A man that truly loves you
Will do just about anything for you

So, if you want a man to love
Be a woman to be loved
You'll never have to worry about life
That's what love is made of

Dignity and Pride

There was a man
Who coached a team?
And didn't say a word

Grumble, grumble
Stomped his feet
Was the only sound heard?

His teams performed
Magnificently
With discipline and poise

The only sound of loosing
Was the sound
Of the other team's noise

He went on to win
Great championships
Turning the heads of many

If he ever made
A mistake in life
I can't remember any

From coaches, and players
To fans, and referee's
It's what all came to expect

Proud and tall
This man stood
Surrounded by respect

I had the chance
To coach at his side
And I really learned a lot

Carry yourself
With dignity and pride
Something I never forgot

Bob Hughes Senior

Do what you can

Do what you can do
And try to understand
The greatest gift in life
Is to serve your fellow man

MLK Jr. spoke these words
And still reign true today
Some people have a hard time
Just making it through the day

People touched your life
As a kid you started to grow
Now the life you live
Is the evidence that you show?

You have something to teach others
No matter what life shows?
Good or bad the life you had
Will inspire others when you go

So, let the life that you live
Be the light for some to follow
Be ashamed if people curse your name
When gone, it's a tough pill to swallow

Do what you can, while you can
We have such little time
Family and friends until the end
Is the legacy you leave behind?

The You Inside of You

There's a you inside of you
Trying to come out
Situations will show you, you
That's what a rearing is about

School, military and the streets
These are your training grounds
Attending one of these institutions
Is where your you will be found

You will have to live with you
No one can be you but you
So, the you inside of you
Is the you based on what you do

It is possible to double up
And you can have all three
The school will give you options
Of what the you in you should be

The disciplined you inside of you
Will bring out the military in you
You'll face life and death situations
To survive the you inside of you

The streets, a whole new game
You're still looking for you
The trouble with this you
You're the you, others see in you

Followers show an insecurity
You're afraid of the real you
Leaders have a certain trait
The you, others see in you

Let's recap the you in you
To see if you're happy with you
Education will induce thought
And the streets will do so to

That's the you raised in you
Someone instilled that in you
Mom, dad or both demonstrate
What that you, need to do

It's up to you to be the you
That will live inside of you
Opened eyes, or closed eyes
You will lay down with you

The mirror shows what you know
Looking at the you inside of you
Smile, frown, or cry your eyes
Will be the you, looking back at you

No one can tell you to be happy with you
That's something only you can do
You'll dictate situations with choices
That's the happy you'll find in you

Live or die you ask yourself, why?
Was that the you in me
You'll find in the back of your mind
Was that the who you needed to be

Happy Fathers-Day 2012

Another Fathers-day
And the texts came rolling in
I thank God every single day
For waking me up again

Then I think about friends
Who've pasted or gone their way
Whose wife and children won't be able to say?
Hey dad happy Fathers-day

I'm blessed to have two sons
Who spent this day with me?
I pray that I'm the type of dad
That they would want to be

It's not always easy
Trying to do the right thing
Especially when you receive ridicule
For the positive things you bring

But they seem to be turning
Into the men I would like to see
Responsible, caring and strong willed
The rest is okay with me

This was a day I'm proud to say
Thanks for another Fathers-day
I await the time when its mine
To say to them, happy Fathers-day

I would like to see what they will be
When they bring up their kids
So, I can look back and say on that day
That's the same thing I did

Hear what I'm Saying

There's nothing like a person
       Who knows how to listen?
When you talk to someone
       Their eyes don't glaze or glisten

They listen to everything
       And can quote back what you say
Coming home to someone like this
       Makes it easy to do the day

They hold you and console you
       To put your spirit at ease
They tell you it's going to be okay
       And to hear this seems to please

They can even empathize
       They know what you went through
This is the kind of person
       That makes it easy for you to be you

So, if you find someone to listen
       Go ahead and bend their ear.
There's nothing like having something to say
       And they hear you loud and clear.

So, love laugh and listen
       And living is what you'll do
It's hard to see where you're going
       If no one is listening to you.

Hopes and Dreams
(The path)

When that door closes on dreams
Will it open again?
That depends totally on you
Will it be you, your will, or man?

When that door opens for you
Will it shine a light?
Will you pray for what you say?
Every day and every night

There're glass doors, brass doors
And doors made of wood
Don't be afraid to walk through
You stand where you stood

If you let others dictate
When to open or close the door
You willingly give up the right
To make decisions any more

You never know what you can achieve
Until you begin to try
When that door finally opens
You'll walk through and know why

If someone turns the knob
Make sure that someone is you
Look through doors, knock them down
Do whatever you need to do.

Inspired

To walk among the birds
You feel like you can fly
Doing things, you didn't think you could
And still not know why

Having the hindsight
To see what others can't see
Achieving the things in life
Not knowing what you want to be

It's like helping other people
With little regard for you
Knowing that your sacrifice
Are things that people do?

They're many different quotes
Inspiring our lives at times
Giving us the will to succeed
When failure clouds the mind

Giving us the sense of mind
To see what others can't see
To feel what others can't feel
So, we can be what others can't be

Ridiculous

What do kids see?
When adults do what they do
Kids are like a sponge
And they soak up what you do

If you walk by someone
And decide not to speak
Children will become rude
And rudeness is what they seek

If you fail to hold the door
And let someone walk in
Children will often follow our lead
And do what we did again

Then comes the final straw
Yes, ma'am and no ma'am
We don't use that at home
That's just the way that I am

We must set the example
For kids to want to aspire
Why should they do what we say?
Knowing that's not what's require

So, if we want kids respectful
Then we must lead the parade
Because kids are only as rude
As the courtesies that we've made

Rough Edges

Rough around the edges
But the woman tends to come out
And when it does, she does
That's what I'm talking about

A smile out of this world
And laughter from the heart
All she wants is to be happy
And that's how we got our start

A firm strong stature
Even better when in heels
A woman defined by beauty
I touched her and yes, she's real

She can be a hand full
In the hands of the wrong man
That's why this precious cargo
Will always be in safe hands

She's not afraid to work
And she's looking for that dream
That dream of happily ever after
Not for shine but for beam

Rough around the edges
And the lady in her won't wear off
No matter how you feel about her
Just don't set her off

When I hold her in my arms?
I can feel her every breath
Embracing her soft gentle lips
A love worthy until death

That Winter Feeling

Romance in the winter
Is always a good time
I know you've heard of fantasies
So, let me tell you mine

Its 32 degree outside
With a slight northern breeze
The ground is partially white
And if you look there are no leaves

The fireplace is crackling
As hickory fills the room
Christmas music is playing
Santa will be here soon

She comes out of the bedroom
With a little red something on
Then we kiss and dance
To our favorite Christmas song

I take a sip of chocolate
She takes a sip of coffee
We look out the window together
As reflections, reflect our we

The warmth from holding each other
Provides a passionate chill
Eye to eye, and breath to breath
Gives us that winter feel

Her Man

Earlism:

4.

A strong woman's love
Is difficult for a weak man
To embrace.

Hand full of wishes

What happens if you
Make a wish
And it never comes true

There was something
You really wanted
But it just wasn't meant for you

A star was falling
Through the sky
So, then you close your eyes

Then it seems
It never came true
Wow, another wish dies

You through a coin
Into a fountain
After you turned around

Then after a few days later
No hopes or wishes
Anywhere to be found

You take a wish bone
Break it in half
What will happen next?

Four fingers and bones
One short, one long
You're on the wrong side of the hex

It seems that when
You close your eyes
Your wishes seem to flash

You want all
Life's to give
But all you yield is trash

Happy and Content

There seems to be this dream
To be happy and content
Sitting on the porch holding hands
Talking about times well spent

Laughing at the hard times
And appreciating the good
Lucky that you found each other
Someone who are both understood

I can see it all now
How this contentment takes place
It's just before the setting sun
Where stars still light up space

You can see the lights move
Streaking through the sky
Listening to the sound of night
As a gentle breeze pass by

The leaves in the trees
Move about with something to say
As they fall and hit the ground
This is the place I choose to lay

You can tell which leaf is female
Because they constantly move
The male leaves stay in one place
A foundation that sets the mood

This is one of the dreams
That plays over and over each night
These types of dreams and fantasies
Take place when things are right

Her Legacy, Her Life

It's hard to watch our elders
Eventually grow old
They began to hallucinate
As the memory grows cold

They just don't move
Like they used to
When we were just kids
There was nothing they couldn't do

Taking care of us all their lives
Now it's finally our turn
To help them grow old gracefully
And show them what we've learned

Then there will come a day
That we must put them away
For they've lived a healthy life
With no regrets, and nothing to say

It saddened my heart
When she spoke of my mom
Who's been dead since 1997?
But she was hoping she'd come

I didn't have the heart to tell her
That mom passed away
I didn't think she needed to hear it
On her 92nd birthday

It's hard to watch older people
Finally grow old
So, live your life and do what's right
She turned 92, I'm sold.

Hurting for Love

A woman with so much strength
She can't afford to be weak
A man will steal your strength
If you appear to be mild and meek

It starts out with signs of disrespect
Then it leads to control
If you don't stop it when it begins
You may or may not grow old

Men will only do
What a woman will allow them to
So, don't blame life on the world
When heartaches began with you

Then when a real man comes along
And touches you the right way
Who wants to take the pain go away?
Embracing the essence of love everyday

Provide and take care of her
Like no man has ever done before
A man that will give his heart
His soul and then some more

The mind is a place to travel
Conversation hot chocolate or wine
Love is what the woman wants
Not just sometimes, but all the time
No matter what

If I could remix

If I could touch your face
I would wipe away your tears
If I could touch your heart
You'd feel a love sincere

If I could touch your smile
Then I could feel you laugh
If I could love any one
I would love you on my behalf

If I could hold your hand
And dance with you all night long
I wouldn't just make you strong
I'd make you, MANning strong.

If I could have your trust
I would constantly protect your heart
Our lives would be revered by all
While loving each other's an art

If I could make our kids
Proud to be proud
And take pride in all they do
And lead a quiet life out loud

If I could do about anything
To share my life with you
Walk side by side, hand in hand
Because that's what MANning's do.

It's Okay to be loved

You shouldn't be afraid
To be loved
Especially when asleep at night

When it's all
You're dreaming of
Love should just feel right

How it feels
To be held
When you need to be held

How it feels
To know they care
You know; because they can tell.

How it feels
To be cuddled
When you don't want to be alone

How it feels
to have someone
Make that house feel like a home

How it feels
To cook a meal
And someone tells you, "Now that's good"

How it feels
To have someone
Understand what you understood

How it's feels
To love someone
Who wants to be loved in return?

How it feels
To have passions revealed
With secrets you've both earned

How it feels
To wake up knowing
Someone will always be there

You have the right
To know that at night
When in sickness someone cares

No one
Should be afraid
Of what they're dreaming of

If that person's
A special person
It's okay, to be in love.

It's Heart to be Invisible

The best part of you
Is not the part they can see?
I can see the part of you
That other men couldn't see

They can see that care in you
And hear in your voice concern
Embracing honesty, you provide
But can't feel a passion that burns

They know that you'll give them
The last dime in your pocket
The shirt on your back may be too small
But if need it be, they can have it

They know that you will lift their spirits
Just by the way you smile
They make appointments they don't need
Just to be near you for a little while

Your co-workers embrace your presence
To help make it through the day
Not knowing that if you didn't work there
You'd do the same thing anyway

So, cross the street or walk a mile
It's just you, being you.
People can't see the size of your heart
But you should know, I do.

Little Piece of Happiness

I don't want a lot
Just a little piece of happiness
Nothing above all others
But it stands out from the rest

That type of traditional love
That was meant to be shared
People did things for each other
For love and because they cared

When dinner used to mean something
When the family sat down to eat
Laugh joke and discuss the day
Looking forward to the final treat

When you work hard all day long
Then come home to the one you love
knowing that when the going gets rough
There's nothing stronger than love

The bond that two people share
When spoken are these vows at hand
The kind of trust that should be shared
Between a woman and a man

So, when I lay me down to sleep
This is what I pray
To have that little piece of happiness
With someone special everyday
I embrace the opportunity
One day it'll be just you and I
In love forever, for always
Until life passes us by

Live to let go

I know you've heard the stories
Of letting go to live
That's how I love my wife
And that's the love I give

When we generally take a walk
I walk next to the street
So, a passing car won't leave a mar
Because my love isn't weak

When we go into a restaurant
I'll always get her chair
Because that's what a husband does
To show his wife he cares

If we were to cross the street
A flood won't touch her feet
The reason you haven't seen it
Is because it hasn't happened yet

I love to spend time with my wife
To have her hand and to hold
I'll rock my chair and her chair too
Our love will never grow old.

Sometimes I sense her happiness
Is not where it's supposed to be?
She doesn't know but I try to show
I love her the way that she loves me

So, I wrote this poem
Not because she's my wife
I wrote it because I love **Sophia**
More than I love life

Sense of Love

Out goes the old
And in comes the grew
Skies once grey
Are skies now blue?

Whenever I take a drink
I can taste her lips
To embrace the breath, you breathe
I drink in little sips

When I'm asleep at night
I can feel you next to me
The thought of you on top
Genially relaxes me

Every song I hear
Remind me of things we did
Your love is like a candy store
And in this store, I'm the kid

I can smell your excitement
With the passing of a breeze
If the way I feel is a sickness
Sign me up for that disease

Sometimes I can hear you call
When I'm walking all along
When I turn around to answer
With no you, the sensation's grown

All I do is close my eyes
And my nose begins to rejoice
All I do his close my ears
And I can see your voice

Mom's Ride

Every mom has that car
They've always wanted to drive
Four speeds or an automatic
Whatever makes them feel alive?

Something they can dress up in
Or just pull back their hair
Go to church or just take a ride
So, their face blows in the air

Turn on and up the radio
Listening to music of choice
Then somewhere along the way
With the world they share their voice

They pack up kids in mini vans
And off to the games they go
Laughing, and singing all the way
"Can I drive says the 10-year-old" NO

Her haven is her ability to leave
To get up and go when she can
Because in the heat of an argument
She's got to get away from that man

Soon enough, when she calms down
She'll make her way back home
Her family is that hidden treasure
That many of us grew up on

The car saved the day, one might say
And preserved their way of life
If she leaves and never comes back
She's probably not a good wife.

So, father when she gets upset
Just let her have her say
The only reason she needs to leave
Is so that she can stay

Husband and Wife

Once there was a fairytale Princess
Sophia was her name
She was drop dead beautiful
Her smile was her claim to fame
            All the villagers loved her
            And would always stop to visit
            She had a heart made of gold
            And her disposition was exquisite

She was in love with a prince
Who would offer her the world?
Not because she was a Princess
But because his name was Earl
            They had magical moments together
            Blessed by the hand of God
            They would go and do just about anything
            No activity would seem odd.

They could sit and watch paint dry
And talk about their day
She would talk and he would listen
Pretending not to hear what she'd say
            She would get upset
            And claim he needs to pay attention
            Prince Earl would truly play his role
            Until there was something to mention

They would soon marry
And take each other's hand
Do you Earl take this woman?
And Sophia takes this man
         To have and to hold
         Until the days you grow old
         Sophia you would do what you're asked
         And Earl do what you're told

The rings were presented
You may now kiss the bride
Even though they were smiling
Both were very grateful inside
         True love seemed to elude them
         In relationships experienced before
         Since man didn't create this union
         They would seek to love no more

A Rose for my Love

I would walk a mile
Just to give my wife a rose
Through the forest on the beach
Walk a mile to twinkle your toes

That mile would include
What it takes to make you smile
It wouldn't take all day long
But it may take a little while

Why would it take so long?
Just to walk this mile
Not everyone you met
Can capture me with a smile

Inside of this mile
I would sing and I would dance
The best part of the mile
Is that I get another chance

To hold her hand, and taste her lips
Would be the treat of the day
With this rose I thee love
It would say what I couldn't say

To love someone
Who loves me back in a mile or two?
I know that I just said one mile
But for you I would walk two.

In this mile there is a thought
That captures the memories of
A woman I met not long ago
That I'm proud to share my love

Awl Man

Earlism:

5.

Eagles

Don't become Eagles

Until they are dropped from the nest.

They can't sit around the nest

Eating up all the worms.

They must catch their own worms.

All My Life

Where've you been all my life?
When I used to close my eyes at night
A heavy heart was filled with pain.
Where tears rolled, no matter how tight

We play and we have fun
You laugh, I laugh, and we laugh
This man once incomplete
Has found his other half

Your spirit is filled with a beauty
And a heart of empathy for the weak
You possess that kind of finesse.
With strength that real men seek

I think of you during the day
And the way you touch the world
Filled with happiness and excitement
With moments that make toes curl

I've always wanted to have this feeling
That I feel whenever I'm with you
With a pair of knees and a prayer
God delivered to me, my Boo

So, every day that I can smile
My heart will warm the sky
Because since you came into my life
Sad times are no longer a sign

So, when I close my eyes at night
Engraved in my pillow is a smile
Put there by the grace of God
Sent special delivery

                    In heavenly style

She's a Jeanious

If we define the word jeanious?
It's someone who personifies jeans
Giving jeans a different look
With words you really don't mean

She can wear them rolled up
Or she can roll them down
Either way you look at it
Amazed is what I'm found

Wear them with tennis shoes
Heels or a pair of vans
Each dictating a certain mood
Unknown to common man

I have that certain insight
Because I see it every single day
I see her in and out of the jeans
A price I'm willing to pay

So, with the jeans and with the shoes
How does she top it off?
With a t-shirt or open blouse
Men stare as if they're lost

A pull over sweat top
For those running errand days
It doesn't matter what she wears
Men still ponder in amaze

She has the brain and brawn
To try any pair of jeans on
Until this day I must say
My breath has never been gone.

Men will ponder and men will stare
At this Jeanious who is my wife
And if you could see what we will be
Then you'd wish you had my life.

Sophia's Secret Seduction

She lays there with a blind fold
Sunny side down
Slowly I caress her spine
Oooh, look what we found

I've never heard that sound before
From a touch and sudden chill
Every touch that I would take
Made it hard for her to keep still

We're going to need new sheets
As she's griping tiny holes
Her back arches to the sky
With a deep curl in her toes

Now she's sunny side up
Wow this woman in stacked
Gasping with anticipation
As the bed teases her back

Now I'm a little excited
You should see my eyes
As I move around the bed
I can see the moist inside

Now my lips have some fun
Starting at her feet
Working my way up her thighs
I can feel her heartbeat

Then the moistness touches my head
As I rise to look
Then my tongue soon discovers
The ground beneath me shook

You won't believe what happens next
It was all of that and then some
But I guess you'll have to wait till later
That's in a poem to come

When Will It Matter?

When will it matter?
This life God gives to you
Mediated by mom and dad
He took time to make you

Parents should help you grow
Into a woman or young man
So that when they're no longer here
You can live and then understand

The world will not wake you up
And casually hold out its hand
If you don't learn how to walk
It will not help you to stand

Mom and dad should leave a path
That you should walk with pride
If you fail to grow and prevail
There's something missing inside

You can't be afraid to take a chance
So, step out onto that limb
You'll have to live with a purpose
Life doesn't happen on a whelm

So, when will it matter to you?
In this world God has given
How can you lead your family?
In a life where you're not driven

Sleep Is a Beautiful Thing

Sleep is a beautiful thing
But it matters where you nod
If you sleep in the wrong place
You may wake up next to GOD

Sleep when you're tired
And to the world dead
You shut out all forms of light
With a pillow on your head

A power nap is always good
In the middle of the day
That little jolt of rejuvenation
Then Bam! You're back on your way

Then there's that sleep at night
When you're ready to go to bed
You hug and kiss your mate good night
But you choose to cuddle instead

Then there's that sleep
Whenever an event takes place
It's funny that the way you sleep
Is the evidence on your face?

Then there's that dangerous sleep
Fall asleep behind the wheel
Wake up with that look on your face
But the incident was for real

So, if you're going to grab some sleep
And gently close your eyes.
The best sleep in the whole world
Is that sleep after babies' cry?

The Conversationalist

It's time to curve the conversation
Men who are no longer kids
You can't just say anything anytime
For something you don't like we did

All that yelling and hollering
Someday won't have a sound
A man should hold his head up
Instead of just looking around

If it continues, you'll look up one day
And find you're standing in a shadow
Of a tone that has no microphone
In the company of others, a widow

If love wasn't the obvious agenda
Then this poem would have no need
So, since it's a conversation you can't hear
Then maybe it's something you'll read

If you want to face the conversation
Whenever words can be told
With yelling, screaming, oh and yelling
Alone will be a new kind of old

So, with this love I you wed
Where the yelling is no longer fed
I re-pronounce you family and family
Conversations should be spirit led

The Value of Being Polite

A younger man once asked me
Why do you say sir and ma'am?
I never tend to be mean or offend
But that's just the way I am

My mom always taught me
To respect the people around me
For they won't know who to show
Until its self-worth they see

It costs nothing to be respectful
Its value cannot be measured
You'll never experience the joys of life
Until you've met someone else's pleasure

Every personal path you cross
Should mean something every day
It matters not what you have or got
Always have something positive to say

People don't know self-worth at times
Until it is pointed out.
Say it enough they began to believe
Now it's what they're about

That's why yes sir and ma'am young man
Because in life you never know
What someone thinks about themselves?
Respect gives them permission to glow.

Where I'm from.

I'm from that great state
Big, in size and large at heart.
Big in smells, big in sound.
Big in food which is where we'll start.
Dallas in a pretty big city
In a very large state indeed
Drive all day and drive all night,
Still in Texas, even if you speed.

Then you talk about the smell
Hickory burning over a fire
It makes you stop in your tracks
The smell is what you desire

Since were on the subject smell
Let's pause and talk about food
Mom would cook so much to eat
Not to offer you any would be rude

Barbeque ribs, chicken and links
Grilled to a tender brown
Your taste buds know what good is
Ummmmmmm is the only sound.

Live bands play at night
Country, Jazz, and R & B
Sipping wine as you dine
A mood you can almost see

Let's talk about the nighttime air
Crickets are off to sleep
In the morning the rooster crows
While standing on his feet.

Dallas Texas, is my home
There's no other place to live.
If you were me, then you'd be
Thanking God for what he gives.

Hey-Ref

Hey ref,
What are you looking at?
Are you from footlocker?
You need to go back

That was a bad call
Really you must be kidding
I know you can do better than that
You should sit where I'm sitting

People make comments like these
And will do it all game long
They're not happy when I'm right
They're not happy when I'm wrong

You've got to respect the fact
They second guess your every call
No matter how perfect you may be
You just can't please them all

Behaviors should be managed
And coaching comments entertained
When the intensity is standing
Enjoy the ride and embrace the game

So just referee the game
The way you played and see it
Players and fans will respect your call
Even if they don't agree with it

Momma Always Said

Momma would always make comments
Salivating the thought of mind
Like when decisions had to be made
The most valuable commodity is time

When a person is tired
And dragging their feet around
Alice Manning would always say
Son if you're tired go lay down

If you need some money
Then save for a rainy day
If you're lost ask somebody
Then you'll find your way

If you want respect
You must give it in return
You can't expect people to give
Something you didn't earn

If she heard your stomach growling
Then get something to eat
If there's someplace you need to be
Then get up and move your feet

The world waits for no one
Get up and find your way
When you're feeling, all dogged out
Every dog has his day

This is what I think about
Whenever I'm feeling alone
When you have no place to go
You can always come home.

Mom's Dynasty

Every time I see a Dynasty
My mom comes to mind
This is what she left to me
When it came to be her time

This was a prized possession
That meant a lot to her
She could have had a Ford
But Dodge is what she preferred

This was the car of her dream
Something she always wanted
Power windows and power seats
This was the car she flaunted

I can remember the first day
She drove home in this car
She had a mustang, and elite
But this was her favorite by far

She didn't have a speck of dirt
The carpet was always clean
Playing her Gospel music
Riding to church and she'd lean

I remember getting in her car
The day after she died
I drove her car back to our house
And on that day, I cried

My best friend passed away
I made sure her car was clean
I know that's the way she'd want it
So, when I got inside, I leaned

So, whenever I see a Dynasty
Memories come rushing in
I think about all the good times
We shared, riding together, back then

1988 4 Door Gold Dodge Dynasty

Softball with a Soul

Softball season is about to begin
ASA, little league and high school too
I've got the best seat in the house
Under skies, God painted blue

Standing in the field
Embracing the dew after dark
Umpiring a fast pitch softball game
At a local neighborhood park

Kids watching their team play
In a game where families have fun
Singing and chanting phrases
While players bat and run

Air fresh and clean
Untainted by cigarette smoke
Hickory smells of grills grilling
After meat is tenderly smoked

Left with a comforting feeling
Wishing that contentment can last
Knowing when you wake up tomorrow
That feeling is now part of the past

Then to wind down the day
Where innings are beginning to end
The best part of the stimulation
Is that next week we get to play again

Still Here

Even though you're gone
Your presence is still here
If I didn't know what I wanted, then
Now it's very clear

I turn on the radio
And from the sounds I hear
When all alone I'm thinking of you
Because you're still here

I went to get something to drink
And there was a bottle of beer
I was able to quench my thirst
But you were still here

I was at a game
And the crowd began to cheer
All I could see was your smile
Because you were still here

When I pulled back the covers
There was a stain from your tear
I didn't want to wash it away
Because you were still here

When we talk on the phone
And sentiments are sincere
I miss you even more
Then I wish you were here

Even though your body is gone
Your spirit is still here
Even when I close my eyes
A vision of you appears

I can smell you scent
With every toss of the wind
I can hear your laughter
Then you're here all over again

Daddy's Little Girl

Every now and then in life
Loved ones must depart
Blessing our lives all their life
Now there's a space in our heart

The good old days we celebrate
And all the fun you had
Nothing can replace the smiles
On a face put there by a dad

Tucking you away in bed
Comforting us from our fears
Holding tight to that day or night
When that comfort turns into tears

Heavy are the hearts we carry
Struggling to live in this world
There's nothing in life stronger
Then a bond between dad and his girl

After touching many lives
And blessing the hearts of many
Of all the things in life to regret
We pray he didn't have any

We know he's in a better place
But his memories live on inside
God works hard every day and night
Now there's another angel by his side

The Best Part of the Cookie

Have you ever saved a cookie?
So, you could eat it later
Then when you go back to eat it
You find crumbs, there was a hater

You thought you had it locked away
But someone found the key
Yeah it was just one cookie
But it was a cookie that belonged to me

It was only one cookie
So, there wasn't enough to share
If you wanted a cookie that bad
You should have found one elsewhere.

Then when you go to finish the rest
It just doesn't taste the same
You wonder if they left germs behind
On this cookie that had your name.

It's hard to look at certain people
You're always looking for crumbs
This was your most prized cookie
But somebody else had some.

This cookie you thought you had
Was locked up and put away.
This cookie you just couldn't wait to eat
Waiting at the end of the day

But when you walk through the door
You felt like home just wasn't home
Because someone else tasted your cookie
Now the best part of the cookie is gone.

The Country in Me

I'm often reminded of my youth
When everyday things occur
Smell, taste, and touch
Brings me to things I prefer

Like the smell of hickory burning
Down home Bar-B-Q's
Gathering hands and saying grace
That's what grateful families do

Seeing the look on everyone's face
That's what I enjoy
We didn't know it but back then
Laughter was our toy

Old people racing the young
Skinning up their feet
Upset because the shoes didn't work
Grown-ups would hate to get beat

After they would finally win
Stories were soon to follow
Listening to the excitement in their voice
Made the food easier to swallow

I miss those days way back then
The laughter and the smiles
Wild roosters and rattlesnakes
Memories that stay for a while

A salami and egg sandwich for breakfast
Took me there today
I'm just a good old country boy
What else can I say?

The Man

Earlism:

6.

Nothing in life
Is ever final
Until you stop trying.

Pride of the Eagle

The Eagle drops it young
Expecting them to fly
If they fail to flap their wings
The Eagle will not cry

Sensing they're not ready yet
They scoop them from the sky
Giving them another chance
Like we must walk they fly

They should fly like humans walk
Then later learn to glide
A skill this is difficult to teach
It's why they glide with pride

When the Eagle feeds its young
It drops a worm into the nest
Until it's time for them to fish
Then they can pass that test

Teaching them to fish then to hunt
It can be dangerous hunting snakes
Fishing helps to master the swoop
Then it's a chance they take

Eagles when born open their eyes
Seeing the world from on high
We don't know from down below
When it'll be our turn to fly

Eagles will fly with heads held high
Into clouds of an open abyss
I'll bet somewhere an Eagle cares
Writing them a poem like this

Must Be Hard Being You

It must be hard being you
Being all cool and things
Going to work every day
With that paycheck you bring

You get up in the morning
And head out on your grind
Taking care of you wife and kids
Is the only thing you have in mind?

Will they eat will they sleep?
Do they have a place to stay?
This is the reason you go to work
Every single day

Then when you get home
And the kids are ready for bed
Taking time to comfort minds
Praying before they lay their heads

Thanking God for health and strength
And the blessing of another day
That your family will continue to walk
And show the world God's way

Your wife has dinner waiting
That she cooked with loving hands
So, they you would be revitalized
She appreciates you for being the man

But of course, it's hard being you
Because that's what men do
You should know that when I grow
I want to be just like you.

An Empty Gift

My son exchanged gifts one day
In 3rd grade with other kids
The reason this poem is special
I wasn't proud of what he did

The book he received from another kid
Was a book he already had?
He looked at the book "I have this one"
His ungratefulness prompted a sad

Even though he was eight years old
At home this message wasn't taught
Some people aren't as blessed as others
So, appreciate whatever is brought

The teacher called us at home that night
And told us what he did
We got upset at what we heard
This is more than a kid being a kid

For Christmas he got an empty box
To open on Christmas day
He was excited to receive his gift
The emptiness left him this to say

Hey, this box is empty
Why isn't there anything inside?
We said the box is filled with blessings
And sometimes they tend to hide

The lights, the water, the roof over head
Is something God helps us provide?
So, when you opened that box
That's what you should see inside

That little boy gave a gift
That you tossed against the wall
He gave what he was able to give
So be lucky you got anything at all
He looked at us with tears in his eyes
And said guys I understand
That day even at eight years old
Our son moved closer to a man

So, when we gave him his gifts that day
His appreciation for life was clear
He enjoyed his gifts and played with them
Apologies later were heartfelt and sincere

Today he's graduating from college
He wants to teach and change lives
Today he's able to look in that box
And truly see what was inside.

The Proud Dad

Corroborating Circumstances

People tend to care too much
Putting their heart on the line
Hoping to change just one life
And know everything will be fine

Some people aren't so lucky
To have someone to care
No one left to meet at home
And no one knows you're there

Oh, what a feeling it is
To be loved by someone
To know that when the day is over
You're their number one

The simplest things mean so much
Just sitting and watching T.V.
Enjoying the pleasant company
This is how life should be

A shoulder to cry on
When you have a reason to be sad
Someone to cheer for you
Whether you're doing good or bad

Someone to finish sentences
Before they even began
Pretty soon when you both pray
You look at each other and say amen

There's nothing in the world
Like having a support system in place
Someone who always has your back
Your front, your side, and your face.

Deaf-nently Love

When two people are in love
Deaf love can mean so much
Everything in life has meaning
Every sign, smell, and touch

You can truly appreciate everything
Surrounded by the senses and more
Seeing life in a whole new arena
Like you've never experienced before

Flowers, trees and leaves
Makes you appreciate the breeze
Sensations of the wind on your face
Can place the mind at ease

The simple things mean a lot
Like how they smile and gesture
Sign language and expression
Emphasized by passions and pleasures

I can't imagine what it is like
But it can happen to us all
To not be able to hear anything
Even your name being called

When two people are in love
They find a way to communicate
Love is truly a beautiful thing
When people find a way to relate

Kiss and Tell

A kiss will generate emotion
Created from hearts and minds
It will tell you all the secrets
Every single time.

You can't hide emotions
From the passions of a kiss
Even with the eyes close
They're chills the body won't miss

Going through the motion
Made through likely sentiments
How does one tell the difference?
Redundancy must be evident.

Let's put this to the test
How can you test a kiss?
Not from stealing or in passing
It can't be tested like this.

When emotions are reciprocated
Open is the heart and mind
You just can't hide what's inside
Even from a man that's blind

This is how it starts
So, listen if you please
The lips gently touch
As if to slowly blow on leaves

Not too dry, not too wet
Just enough to make them damp
Your arms are their protection
Escaping that loneliness stamp

Passionate are your breaths
When closed are the eyes
Feel the flow of emotion
Moving freely through her thighs

Things start to awaken
That's been dormant for some time
This is how you test a kiss
It works every single time

This way you can be assured
Of what's inside the heart
A feeling that is fact or fake
It's how you tell them apart.

Disappointing Children

The sound of disappointment
Is when you let a child know?
You're disappointed in them
Displeasure on their face shows

They didn't do their best
And their efforts were the results
You expected more than they gave
As they embrace that look of fault

Without you having to say a word
The kids will buckle down
You must show them that you care
For their efforts are to be renowned

It's okay to have a relationship
One of adult and a child
Never let that line be crossed
And they'll go that extra mile

So, let a child know you care
And that you always expect more
Then step back and watch them shine
Like they've never shined before

Good for the Ego

I was shooting baskets one day
And made a couple of shots
The more my students cheered
I kept shooting and couldn't stop

Following through dance on one leg
They went in again and again
One basket after another
They just kept on going in

When you do things kids can't do
They tend to cheer you on
Not knowing before you did it right?
You had to do it wrong

Kids want and need an idol
And they're generally good for the ego
While adults know what you can do
Kids are in awe of what you know

Then when they have the chance
To plant that know how seed
Now they look to be cheered on
As they grow, and they succeed

Looking to you to get it right
And kindly show them the way
This is what they look forward to
Day, after day, after day

So, if a role model is what they need
Then that's just what I'll be
Because when I was just a child
I remember what my role model meant to me.

Grown Man Stuff

A grown man goes to work
Each and everyday
He goes to work when it hurts
That's the grown man way

Be ye tired or be ye sick
The bills will never end
Because if you don't go to work
Your next will never begins

You must pay your car note
Walk or Uber the ride
You must take care of yourself
Responsibility will not hide

What about a place to stay?
You must lay your head
You can't say you didn't know
Make good decisions instead

Grown man stuff can be tough
Persevere when times are tight
Grown man stuff will keep you up
You just can't sleep some nights

You'll be alone when we're gone
Grown men must grow up.
Put away toys as little boys
Grown man stuff will fill up cups

The time to cry will pass you by
When the grown man stuff kicks in
You'll begin to see what life will be
Now you're grown, life can begin.

I Love you Jaelen

My son cried on my shoulder last night
For he didn't know his worth
I told him how much his dad loved him
The most important thing on this Earth

I could tell he wanted to give up
But I won't let that be
You have way too much to live for
If you could see what I see

Just because the sky is cloudy
Doesn't mean the sun won't shine
You are going to be alright
You're a Manning and a son of mine

We don't give up on anything
And we will never quit
If there is a time for you to shine
Then this time is it

Trust is going to be the key
All you must do is believe
Trust in God when against all odds
And it's his mercy that you'll receive

Thank you, son, for trusting me
With tears you had to shed
My wife and I will continue to try
To man-size you till God nods his head

Continue to try as time goes by
You'll be loved and often admired
Don't stop when you think you had enough
"You stop when the Gorilla gets tired"

Leaders of Success

Success has a downside
You can sometime stand alone
No one really cares about you
All they want is your throne.

They pretend to be happy for you
While envying you inside
While they stand there clapping out loud
Deep down they wished you died

"How did they get so lucky?
That should have been me"
They don't see the labor pains
The baby is what they see

They don't see the sleepless nights
The tossing and turning in bed
They see the money fame and glory
And still they wish you were dead

Yes, success is a lonely road
Especially when you succeed
Whenever you're around people
Automatically you take the lead

We don't have a problem
Stepping out on that leadership limb
At some point you're no longer leading
Now you're carrying them

Still it's not a problem
Because that's what leaders do
If you haven't stood alone in success
There'll be days it'll happen to you.

Limited by Dreams

When I look at kids today
Their lives have no limit
They will only get out of it
Whatever they put in it

Success is what we teach
But what do children learn
Will what they know at home
Surpass our respect they earn

Whenever kids go to school
They should see success
How we walk, how we talk
Our demeanor and our dress

When they look at us
Is us who they want to be
Are will they find another model
More interesting than you and me

We are all in this together
To help them reach the sky
Dreams of success have no limits
They will surely ask questions why

We are all in this thing together
From their beginning to our end
They should know their lives will start
Whenever they start to put in.

Moments in a Day

Every night since we met
Magic has turned the page
Now I feel passion and gentleness
Where there used to be rage

A soft-spoken voice
On the other end of the phone
Told me it's okay to love
And I don't have to live life alone

I know that God answers prayers
And does it in due time
He knew when I would be ready
Body, heart, and mind

If anyone ever wanted to know
What is happiness like?
Depending on how much time you have
It would probably take all night

If you want to know what it's like
To hold someone and be held back
All you do is look in their eyes
And feel them looking right back

When you're holding each other
And the moments escape the night
When heads hit the pillow
It will be peace, gratitude and
                    The subtleness of the night

The Girl behind the Child

Today I had a little girl
Touch my heart and soul
Betrayed by the ones she loved
How can family be so cold?

Taking away that innocence
Love was their disguised
The ones that should protect her
Were the ones who told her lies.

When she closes her eyes
The world will never be the same
Uncomfortable with some conversation
Her world is filled with shame

Not knowing how to feel
And you can see it in her eyes
The way she now acts in class
Screams out in a personal cry

Confused by appropriateness
Because someone planted that seed
She cries down deep inside
Afraid to ask for what she needs

She has so much to offer the world
Even though the thoughts remain
She should know she is seen
Through all her hurt and pain

Yes, my heart cries out for her
Her safety stolen from home
She should know how to be a child
Instead of what it's like to be grown

Who can she talk to?
Will she have a place to run?
She should know her voice is heard
And Gods will, shall be done.

Pictures of Her

A picture-perfect image
Seems to come to mind
Whenever I think of her
Each, and every time

I can picture an angel
Floating on heavens cloud
I can hear her voice singing
When the silence is loud

I can see her smiling
When humor befalls the ear
I find a reason to make her laugh
Her happiness I long to hear

I can see her lying in bed
The night embraces her eyes
When she sleeps her pillow weeps
That's when my heart sighs.

I can sense her presence
Whenever I feel a breeze
I can sense her touch
When I'm down on my knees

When I think about forever
And how forever can be
I can see us together forever
I picture us now as we

Real Love

Real love doesn't hurt
And comes without any pain
It doesn't take a lot of work
And in love you shall remain

All it takes is giving your heart
Your mind body and soul
Love given in this manner
Its love that never grows old

The same page every day
And every night you vibe
The kind of love everyone knows
Every moment you're alive

God has touched your spirit
To begin a brand-new day
Blesses that union with his love
As you both go about your way

To help improve the quality of life
Of those who cross your path
Two people's kindred spirit
This is called God's math

A love that's not boastful
Everyone just happens to see
How in love you truly are
That's the way love should be

If someone ask it's not a secret
Just tell them how it feels
So that they can see with their eyes
That true love can be real

All the Real Dad's

Some guys don't have a dad
That will answer when they call
A dad that will help them stand
Whenever they should fall

A dad that will be there
To help them dry their tears
A dad who has always been there
For years and years and years

A dad that will show them
How to change a flat
A dad that will help them manage
When the dog chases the cat

A dad that will advise them
No matter how much it hurts
A dad that will show them
To get a job and go to work

A dad that will show you things
That will make a man a man
A dad to help you answer questions
Whenever you don't understand

When it seems that all your friends
Are laughing more than you
You should always keep this in mind
They have problems at home to.

When you're feeling all alone
And your head just won't raise up
When it seems, life is escaping you
With God by my side and phone
I will always pick up

That Proud Feeling You Get

There's another feeling you get
That makes your chest rise
It happens when something takes place
And you just can't believe your eyes

It's like seeing a mirror image
Of the things you used to do
And sit and watch someone do it
Just the way that you used to

The words that come out
The intensity that follows
The emotion felt by all who watch
And all you can do is swallow

Time outs called
At the right time and place
Then watch the player's response
There's a certain look on your face

The bench is getting hard
And you haven't been there long
But this is one of those moments
That you feel you just belong

You waited all your life
Just to see what your kids will be
And in this moment of the game
My son was just like me

The way the kids called his name
Coach what do we run?
All I could do proud and true
Was sit back as say that's my son?

Amen

Earlism:

7.

Anything you can do
GOD can do better.

The Good Sleep

Have you ever closed your eyes?
And didn't want to wake
The comfort of your sleep
Endorse the dreams you make

Your body was so at rest
With a complete presence of peace
All the tensions of the world
And the day were suddenly release

Where you laid was warm and cozy
Smothered in your bedding
Never thinking for one second
That death is where you're heading

A sleep that felt so good
That you didn't want to open your eyes
Dreams and memories flood the mind
As your fantasies reach the sky

How did you spend your day?
Did you leave things better than found?
Did you touch another person's life?
So that now you can lay you down

So now whenever you find the time
Or whenever you fall asleep
If you should pass before you wake
It's your soul that God will keep

Who has the time?

Father time has other kids
One is named no time at all
He doesn't really weight much
And doesn't stand very tall

When faced with a task at hand
He never seemed to be around
It almost like he's hiding
And never anywhere to be found

His other brother's Time to finish
And you have too much time
One seems to always rush through things
The other has a lot on his mind

Then you have time to go
And you have time to stay
One is always in the streets
The other doesn't care either way

Then you have time for this
And you have time for that
Finding everything in the world to do
While wondering where you're at

Then you have time to change
And you have time to be mature
It's really time to be your self
In times when you're unsure

It's time for you to pay attention
Especially in times like these
If you didn't know his oldest son
It's time to get on your knees.

The Faithful

What does your morality scale?
Show when it is measured
Does it yield an honorability?
Protecting things, you treasure

Does it show a question mark?
When thoughts sometime wonder
Does it reveal that character?
With the emotional stress you're under

Does integrity tip the scale?
When temptation catches the eye
Does it hold a sigh of regret?
Leaving you to ask yourself why

What do you see when not with me?
And the offers start to come in
To be with them her or him
Thanks for the offer, but I'm taken

Faithful are we, this you and me,
Morality measures our trust
It's important for you what I do
Happiness isn't convenient, it's a must

So, what does your morality measure
When the results are tested
How is your relationship with God?
By faith are you invested

This Side of the Sand

Every side has a side
So, you will need to choose one
Depending on where you choose to stand
Will determine if you've won

There's this side of the story
It's always different from the other
So, don't take anyone's word
Not even that of your brother

Every contest has a side
One loses and the other shall win
Like life in order to be successful
You must train all over again

Then you have a side you sleep on
Your left side and your right
One side more comfortable than the other
Sometimes you sleep through the night

So, if you're going to choose a side
Make sure it's the one you chose
There's a right and wrong side of justice
Make sure your side doesn't loose

Then there's one side you want to be on
And that's this side of the sand
For if you're on the other side
Someone has bowed their head and hands

This Man I Know

I still hear talk of a man
Who lived long ago?
A man who did great things
And didn't need gratitude to show

There was talk of his miracles
And the special things he did
Let me tell you about this man
What he did for you, me, and kids

Once you experience these things
Suddenly you become a witness
Born or enduring such affliction
The healed have suddenly been blessed

People who were blind
Can now see the sun rise
We are all reminded of this
Each morning when we open our eyes

He healed people who were sick
And made them well again
Cancer kills people every day
Still we deny this man

What about diabetes
The eventual killer of them all
When God fed the multitude
He proved no feet is too small

Water into wine, walking on water
And the dead got up and walked
He didn't ask for much except
To believe and listen when he talks

He provided to us a book
With words printed in red
To prove to us and the world
Through faith he's not dead

So, whenever you see the sun rise
The moon shall fall at night
Just keep in mind his forgiveness
And why we should all do what's right

A Passion for Christ

Emotions are a powerful tool
They control our very being
When you observe someone laughing
Emotions are what you're seeing

When something crosses their path
And tears fill the wells of their eyes
It's because emotions are so strong
That tears can't stop the cries

The love of a God
Can make you fall on your knees
Rejoicing saying thank you lord
Use me any way you please

They're many things that you can do
That make you a fool for Christ
I can think of a reason to pray
When eternity is the ultimate price

So, if you're going to serve the lord
Serve with passion when you do
You may not know what others go through
But you know what he's done for you

Blessed to be

I'm blessed to be able to walk
When I see people in chairs
Chairs that have wheels that roll
At some point you know God cares

I'm blessed to be able to see
When I see people with a cane
Some people need a dog
With the life they have that remains

I'm blessed to be able to feel
Reach out with a helping touch
Blessed to still have this sensation
Because God loves us that much

I'm blessed to be able to talk
When I see those without speech
They have so much to say.
Whenever we hear God teach

I'm blessed to be able to hear
For this is how faith is derived
I'm blessed to have all these blessings
By the grace of God, we shall abide

Diamonds in a Crown

Everyone may not see your work
But God knows what you do
Every time you touch a life
It's a diamond in a crown for you

You will travel a lonely road
Looking for company along the way
Company that won't be there with you
When you have those stand-up days

When a child is disrespectful
Correct them and make them think
Make them understand that in life
Attitudes can make you swim or sink

They should always respect their parents
And know the difference in their words
Some parents are children themselves
Not knowing what was said is what was heard

Choose the people you associate with
Just like you choose your greens
Don't take the first bunch you come across
They may not taste just like you dreamed

So, when it comes to changing lives
Take the road no one else will choose
If it makes another life better
In God's eyes you just can't loose

When a decision must be made
Keep your head up, not down
Your head will need to be held high
To receive diamonds in your crown

Fairy Tale Waiting to Happen

A fairytale waiting to happen
Prince Earl and Princess When
This is not your normal story
So, you won't hear this story again

There won't be any kissing frogs
And no apple to put you to sleep
No kids in a gingerbread house
Or princess kept in the dragons keep

There is one thing our Story will tell
It's a true love forever and after
There'll be hearts that smile
Embraced by love and laughter

I will rescue you from your day
And put on my magic cape
Dazzle you with a sense of humor
That will force the mind to escape

I will protect you from the night
And all the fear it holds
Our love will be a story blessed
That forever will be told

I will sweep you off your feet
Because that's how romance is done
Carry you away in my arms
With a kiss to say you're the one

Living happily ever after
Prince Earl and Princess When
Written by the hand of God
You won't hear this story again

Dedicated to my wife Sophia L Manning

How God Answers Prayers

God has always answered our prayer
Definitive for what we need
No, wait, and yes
Are the answers to our seeds?

He tells us no because we're not ready
To handle if he says yes
We'd hurt ourselves or even others
Creating an even bigger mess

He tells us wait when we ask
Timing with him is a big thing
When it's time he'll tough our minds
With blessing only, a God can bring

Then when it's time for him to say yes
We'll know why he said no
It's not for us to question why
When he loves us enough to say no?

We can't just ask him for anything
When wants are greater than needs
Giving us what we need when he wants
So, in our hearts and minds we feed

He will always answer your prayers
Whenever down on your knees
A casual prayer will get you there
Just ask him and say please

Introducing God

How do you know the Lord?
Did you meet him at an early age?
Did you read about him in a book?
In the bible while turning the page

How do you know there is a God?
When it's someone you never met
How do you find out who he is?
It's something you must go get

You won't get it in the streets
Or by listening to gospel on the radio
It won't come Sunday morning
When you're getting in from a disco

Every pastor has a message
Is his fountain blessed with a glow?
You can't drink water from a dirty glass
Because the ring around it will show

Yes, you did the Sunday school thing
And even sang in the choir
You've memorized the Lord's, prayer
But what is truly your spiritual desire

If you wake up every morning
You have an idea who he can be
Once you find out who he is
There'll be things you'll want to see

You met God at an early age
That's what your parents do
You must truly find a house of GOD
You'll meet him that I promise you

Missing out on Happiness

In the very beginning
God created man then woman
Two people to share everything
With a place for both to stand

Marriage is a communion
Where God puts things together
You miss out on that happiness
When there's one without the other

Then when you're all alone
And a piece of your life dies
Life takes on a whole new meaning
Wondering the answers to why's

Is there going to be a time
When God calls your name
You'll see other happy couples
And think I had the same

We've all gone down on our knees
And asked God to send us the one
Allowing love to touch our hearts
Until our days are done

We all face the fears
Of falling short of life's success
But life can be a little more bearable
When embracing that happiness

So live life with no regrets
Encompassing the pleasures of life
So, when God sends you the one
You can welcome matrimony,
                          As husband and wife

                              Inspired by Unanswered Prayers

Personal Praise

It's okay to personally praise
If that's what you want to do
God touches many lives
You know what he's done for you

Even if you're sitting at work
And suddenly you wave your hand
Because something woke you up
You truly that God is the man

You can be walking down the hall
Then suddenly you skip a step
Because through the grace of God
We know that Jesus wept

You go to the restroom at work
And in the mirror do a dance
Because you knew that all along
God would give you another chance

Things looked bleak, now they shine
At times you fall on your knees
God pulled you out of the darkness
So, the Lord is there any way you please

There's just so much to be thankful for
You can take all day to praise
Make it personal because God is personal
So, take a knee, and bow your head,
                             Every time you pray.

Really! You can't hear God

When God is angry and upset
People and places change
When earthquake moves the ground
Entire continents are rearranged

If we equate that to education
The earthquake is the eraser
Then in comes the tsunami
Simulating a huge sweeper

Of course, you know the tornado
Is when he points his finger?
Hurricanes are just the proof
Of how God's anger still lingers

When sharp brisk wind appears
Seventy-five miles at best
We feel a deep sigh from God
Again, we've failed his test

People are going to get the picture
If they don't then someone will
I'm listening to his anger intently
Because I know how his anger feels

We've only heard about volcano's
With the fire, ash, and heat
If he takes off his RING OF FIRE
They'll be new ground beneath our feet

Simply Put

When we're born
Into this world
Naked birds of J
No one knows
What tomorrow brings
Or how to live each day

All we do
Is live our lives
Hopping for the best
Making decisions
One by one
To get along with the rest

Then we teach them
About a legacy
Dreaming like we did
We fall in love
And marry someone
Next thing you know, kids

Enduring pains
And many pleasures
That life sends around
Broken hearts
Solaced minds
Comfort is to be found

Education an important tool
God's word
Our family and friends
Carries us
Throughout our lives
Hoping for peace in the end

Thank God for Giving

God if this is where you want me
Please let me know
You know I've been a lot of places,
Places I didn't need to go

I haven't always made decisions
In accordance to your commandments
Thank you for your forgiveness
And for a woman that's heaven sent

I pray I mean as much to her
As she does to me
Even with our eyes wide open
We're not always able to see

What is it you'd want for me?
And what will you have us do?
I know that without your grace
We wouldn't be here without you

Bringing us through the pains of life
Where hearts can be deceived
We never stopped trusting in you
When you made it easy to believe?

That there will be something special
In our hearts, our souls, and mind's
That's why if this is meant to be
We give thanks, this is our time

What a time to find each other
During this thanksgiving holiday
Walk with us and talk with us
As we venture down a righteous way

Thanks, Be Given

Breakfast of a champion
Bacon eggs and pancakes
Man, it sure goes down great
For my hands had the make

Enjoying breakfast on the patio
An early morning cool breeze
Sharing moments of intimacy
With the kind of weather to please

Polite conversation
Exploring each other's mind
The best is yet to come
And will come in due time

When I looked into her eyes
Spirits are finally breaking free
A spirit locked away by loneliness
Then God gave me the key

I embraced the task jumped right in
It started over dinner for two
It only got better down to the letter
Comedy was the next thing to do

We laughed till we cried
Then cried till we laughed
Our hearts and minds intertwined
The possibilities of a better half

This would be a fabulous start
A nice means to an end
When most people's life would stop
Ours is about to begin.

Thanks Be to Thee

Well what do you know?
     It's my birthday once again
I've been blessed with another year
     Thank you oh Lord Amen

You know what's in my heart
     And you know who I want to be
I want to take this time to say
     Thank you for the thought of me

I intend to live each day
     To honor and appreciate your name
I know you didn't have to
     But you made me just the same

I know you expect a lot
     From the children of your flock
And I don't want to let you down
     Unlike most I never forgot

The place from which you brought me
     In this life where I first began
Watching over me since I was a child
     Molding me into this man

So, whenever I get the chance
     To thank you for your begotten son
I will also remember to thank you
     For me and everything you've done

The Be in Me

Could there possibly be
Someone out there just like me
Who wants the same things I do?
With the same dreams as me

Will she feel?
The way I feel
Searching for an emotion
Honest sincere, and real

Someone who shares a fantasy
To make that dream come true
Someone who wants to be in love
And make love the way I do

Someone to share a song
That the radio will embrace
To know that when we hear it
A smile will light up our face

To know that when I touch her
She'll be consumed by a lust
For with every breath she takes
Every want becomes a must

Then when we hold each other
Our arms will warm our hearts
It's not all that governs a relationship
But it's certainly a great start

Then comes the hard part
Can she cook, can she clean
Can she make our home a home?
Can she dance when we sing?

Can she make me feel?
As if I'm the last man on this earth
If I can find a woman like that
I'll make sure she knows her worth

Then comes the final straw
To support that camel's back
Will she walk and pray with me
We'll both know that faith is FACT

Hit and Run

I just remembered why
Softball is so much fun
I saw a player milk the pitch
Until she found the one

When she hit the ball
It came off the bat just right
She hit the ball so hard and high
It got lost up in the lights

Her team-mates cheer and shouted
She rounded all the bases
Looking up into the stands
To embrace family and fan face's

I get the chance to ump this game
And watch these players play
Then I realize how lucky I am
Not everyone can hold on to this day

As the night befalls the field
The grass yields to dew
This is when you say amen
There's nothing God can't do.

Where did all the real me go

Where did all the real men go?
Is there a place where they now reside?
Where's that family foundation?
Is there a place where the real men hide?

The place where they hang their hat
Is it the same place they hang their pants?
How do they put on their shoes?
Do they walk or do they prance?

Where do they hang their head?
Is there a ground nearby?
Where's the pride that used to abide
It wasn't that easy to cry

Where is that disciplined man?
Kids would respect what they say
They'd go out ahead of the family
Kids came home at the end of the day

Where is that man of thought?
Who's always ahead of the game?
This man of pride is hidden inside
Now won't answer to his own name

Where did the man go with a heart?
To care for his fellow man
Help me find this man of shine
So, he'll know just where to stand

Where did the man with vision go?
Who could see that brighter tomorrow?
A man to be seen in that Christian mien
Who no longer needs time to borrow?

Blessed are the Grateful

A sun that rises in the east
And it sets in the west
They two times in a day
We see nature at its best.

If we look out over
A wide stretch of land
We can see what happens
When God waves his hand

When he stretches to yawn
We feel a cool breeze
When the devil plants twigs
God sprouts up trees

Miracles created
With only six days passed
He sprinkled out dirt
And up came grass

He threw up the skies,
And laid down the seas,
Then he set aside time
And created you and me

With all these miracles
That occurred in a few days
Don't you think it's time?
We make him proud of what he's made.

Enough Said

I just can't say enough
About how much I love my wife
Next to God she's everything
My best friend, my love, my life

We do so many things together
Like cooking healthy at night
We say grace before we eat
So that everything with God's right

God can truly answer prayers
As he does time, and time again
It's like this prayer was answered
Before I could say amen.

We have so much fun together
And even with our ups and downs
We find our way back to each other
And never lay down with a frown.

I make the bed she tells me how
Pointing her finger to instruct
If you want a woman almost like mine
Keep praying and God was my luck

She teases me with her smile
As she casually walks on by
All I can say is "look at you"
Her laughter is my reply

Then when we dance and sing
We both can sing and dance
The music and moment will pull you in
So, we embrace a special romance

The next time when you're online
Searching for your spouse to be
Bow your head on bending knee
And you'll find a blessing,
                    Just like me.

When God is good

There were times the lights came on
When I struggled to see
Making a way out of no way
God did that just for me

I was stuck in sticky situations
Places I didn't need to be
I found myself back at home
God was watching over me

I even had times in my life
When I struggled to speak
God gave me something to say
So that I wouldn't appear weak

God showed me a person once
Who was living in my house?
When the right woman comes along
I would be a better spouse

You can probably guest as well
With the food and a thirst
God always provided a way
For me to put my family first

So, do I send him up a prayer?
Yes, every single day
Even the days I slip and forget
He still covers me any way

Mom being the women she was
Introduced my God to me
Bless her soul she was told
Heaven is the place to be

So, when I'm lost and all alone
In my heart and mind, I pray
I know that if he's not in my life
I would certainly lose my way

Things I wouldn't want to be

I wouldn't want to be a floor
Because people walk all over you
I wouldn't want to be a microphone
Because you take too much lip too

I wouldn't want to be a door
People don't care to respect you
I wouldn't want to be a tree
Because even birds peck on you

I wouldn't want to be a balloon
People can make your world go pop
I sure don't want to be a garbage can
Putting up with all that trash and slop

I wouldn't want to be a fire hydrant
It's a place where dogs go to pee
I wouldn't want to be a walking cane
Because really, they can't see

Some people don't want to be responsible
Afraid of things they must do
And if this is something you don't want to be
Then I sure don't want to be you

Earlism

If the door is close, kick it open.
If it still doesn't open use two feet.

A married person who will cheat with you,
Will cheat on you.

There is no substitute for respect.

Friends who don't endorse your marriage
Shouldn't be a part of your circle.
In the end all they want is a piece of your
Wedding cake.

The brightest star in the room,
Doesn't always shine the brightest
Until the light goes out.

God will show you who you really are.
If you're willing to except his disclosure?

A woman needs to feel loved and protected.
You can't have one without the other
And keep your women.

A man can't appreciate his journey until he can embrace the road that
he has to travel.

Even with all the family support and advice
People will still struggle to get out of their own way.

Curiosity is the foundation for creativity
Everything else happens by accident.

Loving yourself allows others
To love you the way you deserve to be loved.

Winning doesn't mean anything,
If it doesn't mean anything to you.

Loosing should never an option unless you make it one.

When EGO's crowd the road to success
Pride will suffer the journey.

If you don't teach kids how to be independent
They will spend the rest of their lives being a dependent.

Wanting to be successful in life isn't enough
You must multiply the desires by your efforts.

You can't use happy and lazy in the same sentence unless you're happy
being lazy.

Don't except well enough as good enough
Be the standard by which greatness is measured.

Happiness has a look on people in marriages,
What does your happy look like?

A book may seem appealing but really isn't a good read. Chapter one
may only be one page.

Marriage is a beautiful thing especially with someone who can see and appreciate it the same way you do.

You can't have big dreams when you're comfortable with NAPS.

A parent that makes excuses for their child will help them
Live up to those excuses.

Appreciation is the cornerstone of success.

Crazy has a limit, but stupid can last forever.

Momma always told me that
Right is right and wrong will never be right.

The best remedy for stupid decisions is to make better choices.

History is always told from the perspective of the winner. What really happened will lye somewhere between
victory and defeat.

Sometimes loving your kids means telling them NO!!!

In the game of life not everyone receives a participation trophy, you must earn your own trophy.

When serving up a plate of conversation make sure the topic is on the menu.

A smart phone is only as smart as the person using it.

You should always expect perfection, if not mediocrity will always prevail.

If you don't learn from your past mistakes your future will be a déjà vu.

Success waits on no man,
But failure is right around the corner.

When you wash the mind with clear thoughts, new ideas seem to prevail.

Anybody can quite so why just be anybody? Be better than that anybody.

Kids will listen if you have their attention, but if you have nothing to say they will fade away.

The saddest thing in the world is when a woman carries the weight of a family.

The only substitute for grateful is appreciation.

Index

A Prayer of Gratitude

Lord God our father, thank you for waking us up this
morning and allowing us to see another day.
Thank you for your grace and understanding.
Please forgive us, our family and friends for our sins.
Thank you for providing us with your insight wisdom and knowledge,
and please help us with our words, our thoughts, and our actions.
If it be your will, we ask you to heal the sick, walk with the
storm victims, and embrace those who have lost loved ones.
We ask that you continue to bless us so that we
may bless others through your blessings.
It is with a humble heart and grateful mind that
we ask for a place in your kingdom.
We ask these and many other blessings in
your name and your son's name.

Amen

CPSIA information can be obtained
at www.ICGtesting.com
Printed in the USA
BVHW071021281119
565084BV00001B/115/P

9 781973 678250